IMAGES
of America

JEWISH
MIAMI BEACH

IMAGES
of America

JEWISH
MIAMI BEACH

Paul S. George and Henry A. Green
Foreword by Jonathan Nelson

ARCADIA
PUBLISHING

Published by Arcadia Publishing
Charleston, South Carolina

Printed in the United States of America

Library of Congress Control Number: 2023937804

For all general information, please contact Arcadia Publishing:
Telephone 843-853-2070
Fax 843-853-0044
E-mail sales@arcadiapublishing.com

Visit us on the Internet at www.arcadiapublishing.com

For my brother Eddie and sister Anna, who, along with me, as children so enjoyed Lummus Park and the warm waters of the ocean just beyond.

—Paul S. George

Dedicated to the memory of the Beth Jacob synagogue congregation, the beating heart of Jewish Miami Beach over decades, and to my dear children, Jordan, Trevor, and Fiona

—Henry A. Green

CONTENTS

FOREWORD

In 1978, I came home to Miami Beach from Gainesville. Part of my daily routine was to walk the beach after work from Lincoln Road to the South Beach Pier. When I got around Third Street and Washington Avenue, there was a building with a magnificent dome. Drawing closer, I recognized that this was Congregation Beth Jacob, my grandfather's synagogue and where my father had his bar mitzvah many years before. I went in and introduced myself to Ruth Gudis, the synagogue's secretary.

On the eve of Rosh Hashanah, I took my place upstairs. The synagogue resembled a palace with beautiful stained glass windows and brass chandeliers. Rabbi Shemayaho T. Swirsky and the cantor, Rabbi Berrinholz, both dressed in white, led the service. The former had been my professor at Miami-Dade Community College several years before.

I quickly became a board member, and later president, involved with the operation and preservation of Beth Jacob. The buildings were old and termite ridden with a leaking roof, and the air-conditioning was broken. One of my responsibilities was escorting and seating special members of the congregation on the High Holiday days, among them Meyer Lansky with his family and Yiddy Blum, once considered notorious Jewish gangsters. Black Cadillacs were parked out front, and men in dark suits stood by as bodyguards.

During the late 1970s and early 1980s, a large part of our male population were World War I veterans. Oftentimes they had fought in opposing armies. On holidays, we provided plenty of liquor post service for a blessing over wine, the kiddush. The memories of many of the old vets would be lit, and the battles that pitted the vets of the Austro-Hungarian Army against the Russians were reenacted. Both the emperor of Austria-Hungary and the czar of Russia were cursed in Yiddish.

Unfortunately, I was too young to remember in person all the hilarious stories about the chickens, post–World War II. Rabbi Menchlikoft ran a chicken kitchen in the back of the synagogue. Every Thursday, members would line up to receive their preordered kosher chickens. Miami Beach had limited access to fresh kosher meat, and Beth Jacob's butcher shop offered the best on the beach.

By the 1990s, the synagogue had few members, and we were not able to continue worship services. Today, with the vision of Dr. Henry Green transforming the synagogue into a museum, the beautiful Jewish Museum of Florida-FIU tells the story of the state's history and preserves Beth Jacob's legacy.

—Jonathan Nelson, president of Beth Jacob Congregation

ACKNOWLEDGMENTS

Four decades ago, the University of Miami (UM) invited me to serve as the director of Judaic Studies. I began a course teaching Florida Jewish history that morphed into a UM project called MOSAIC: Jewish Life in Florida, an exhibit that traveled the state of Florida from 1990 to 1992, with the Soref JCC and Center for the Advancement of Jewish Education (CAJE) as partners. In 1989, MOSAIC also became a nonprofit organization (NPO). As the founding director of MOSAIC, I signed a contract with Congregation Beth Jacob, under the leadership of Beth Jacob's vice president Jonathan Nelson, to lease the synagogue to become the home of the Jewish Museum of Florida-FIU (1992). Paul George was my guide in developing curriculum, walking tours, an exhibit book (1991), and for my biography of Rabbi Leon Kronish and the history of Miami Beach (1995). It is an honor to collaborate with him again.

I am grateful to my son Trevor, who photographed images in the book; assistants Jenny Jacoby and Samantha Clayman at Beth Jacob for their generous support; and to longtime friends who sent images when we reached out—Nan Rich, Elaine Bloom, Russell Galbut, Jonathan Nelson, the Garazi and Kronish families, Stuart Miller, Norma and Michael Orovitz, Jenny Lowhar, Stuart Blomberg, and Ann Bussel. Casey Piket has served as our adept virtuoso in all technological and computer matters. Lastly, many thanks to Caroline (Anderson) Vickerson, Arcadia Publishing, who as our editor displayed ample amounts of support.

Jewish Miami Beach has changed dramatically over the past years. Beth Jacob, the first Jewish congregation, has become a legacy to all those who visit Miami Beach. May Beth Jacob's members' memories and all those who continue to create the colors of Miami Beach be blessed.

—Henry Green, professor of Religious/Judaic Studies, University of Miami

Allow me to echo many of Henry's words. I am delighted that he and I could work together again on another history endeavor. I tip my hat to all of those listed by Henry as instrumental in providing us with the materials and the wherewithal to bring this book to fruition. Without their assistance, we would still be at the starting line. My early work as a historian centered on book-length histories of Mount Sinai Medical Center, Miami Jewish Home and Hospital for the Aged, and Temple Emanu-El. The Jewish story of Greater Miami is powerful and inspiring for its successes as well as for the civic, institutional, and political involvement of a dynamic Jewish populace and its contributions to the betterment of our slice of the subtropics. I am honored to have contributed to this study, for it has provided me with the avenue to thank Jewish Miami Beach for all the opportunities and support they provided me, support offered up with large doses of love.

—Paul S. George, resident historian, HistoryMiami Museum

INTRODUCTION

Beth Jacob, the first synagogue on Miami Beach, is listed in the National Register of Historic Places. Founded in 1927 and opened in 1929 on Third Street and Washington Avenue, the members are the pioneers and founders of Jewish Miami Beach. In its heyday, the synagogue boasted hundreds of members and a social hall brimming with activity. It resonated with an aura of spirituality, stained glass windows sparkling with a spire lit up. The beach community worshipped and were married at the synagogue, students learned at the Hebrew School, and snowbirds living in the Art Deco hotels lined up for Sabbath and holiday services.

Members were the architects of the Art Deco hotels, leading players of the economic growth of the beach; the hospitality, health, and business sectors; its politics; and the drama of untold adventures in spite of gentleman's agreements, "Gentile Only" signs, and conspicuous discrimination. In the 1930s and 1940, Henry Hohauser, ranked as one of the most influential people in South Florida by the *Miami Herald*, designed 100 Art Deco hotels and residences featuring streamlined curves, jutting towers, "eyebrows," and neon. Meyer Lansky, the Mob's accountant who developed a gambling empire, was a member. So too were Jennie and Joe Weiss, who came to the beach in 1913. After running a lunch counter at Smith's Casino, the Weisses opened their restaurant, Joe's Stone Crab, still operated by the family a century later and serving more than 1,000 people daily. Bessie and Abraham (Al) Galbut were members who came in the early years of the Depression and established a 24-hour drugstore/restaurant on Fifth Street and Washington Avenue, a go-to place for local politicians and the first auto tag agency on the beach with a newsstand that provided newspapers in Yiddish and many other languages. They left a legacy that their grandson Russell Galbut has exponentially grown into a real estate development company (Crescent Heights). Baron de Hirsch Meyer, the first president of Mount Sinai, the first campaign chair of the Jewish Federation, and the first Jewish Miami Beach councilperson (1934), was also a member of Beth Jacob.

Beth Jacob was a model for the synagogues and Jewish schools that followed such as Beth Sholom, Temple Emmanu-El, and Temple Menorah, all lying north of Beth Jacob, and those that offered homes to Cuban refugees like the Cuban Hebrew Congregation and Sephardi Temple Moses.

Jewish Miami Beach traces the evolution of Miami Beach through pictures from the southern tip of the island north; from the founding of Miami Beach in 1915 to the end of the 20th century through the Beth Jacob pioneers and their children; the migration of Jews from the northeast, Cuba, and Israel; and Holocaust survivors and Jews displaced from the Arab world. Each chapter chronologically scans a period of beach history, from the earliest Jews arriving to the commandeering of Miami Beach hotels by the Army during World War II, from the boom of the postwar period into the 1950s and through the 1970s to the decline and revival of South Beach and the booming of north Miami Beach. The images tell the story of an epic saga of American Jewish history and the shaping of hotel, real estate, and banking industries with a backdrop for the entertainment world and a tourist mecca with sun worshippers; of the dawn and expansion of Mount Sinai hospital; of the birth, gentrification ("God's Waiting Room"), and comeback of the Art Deco district; and the reincarnation of Beth Jacob as a museum. Each historical era in its own way shaped and continues to shape the city's landscape.

It is the story of sanctuary, redemption, and rebirth as each manifestation—from South Beach and the Fontainebleau Hotel on mid-beach to Bal Harbor and the Sunny Isles in the north—paints a different palette to the colors and story of Jewish Miami Beach.

GLOSSARY

bar mitzvah: The religious initiation ceremony of a Jewish boy who has reached the age of 13. He is viewed as an adult with regard to observing religious precepts and participating in synagogue worship. It is legal adulthood under Jewish law. For a girl, it is bat mitzvah, and the age is 12 or 13.

bimah: An elevated platform in a synagogue from which the Sefer Torah is read.

kiddush: A Jewish benediction and prayer recited over a cup of wine.

klezmer music: A Jewish instrumental musical tradition from Eastern Europe.

Kol Nidre: A Hebrew and Aramaic prayer declaring a release from religious vows and obligations that were made unintentionally or under duress. It is recited in synagogues at the opening of Yom Kippur eve services.

kosher: Refers to a Jewish dietary framework for food preparation, processing, and consumption and the kinds of food eaten.

mitzvot: The commandments in the Torah.

Passover: Biblical commandment to commemorate the exodus from Egypt.

seder: A Jewish ritual service and ceremonial dinner for the first night or first two nights of Passover in commemoration of the exodus from Egypt that fulfills the Biblical commandment.

Sefer Torah: Sefer Torah is a handwritten copy of the Torah, meaning the five books of Moses. It is also known as the Pentateuch.

sukkah: A temporary hut with leaves that is constructed for the Jewish holiday of Sukkot to commemorate the nomadic life of the Israelites in the desert after escaping slavery in Egypt.

Yom Kippur: The Day of Atonement. Yom Kippur is the holiest day of the Jewish year and marks a time for atonement through fasting and prayer.

One

JEWS IN
EARLY MIAMI BEACH

The Congregation Beth Jacob Sunday school class poses in front of the synagogue on Washington Avenue. Teachers can be seen standing in the back row. The founding of Congregation Beth Jacob in 1927 marked the first Jewish religious institution on Miami Beach and became the model for the synagogues and Jewish schools that followed in subsequent decades. Many of the students comprising this class were members of the pioneering families who settled south of Fifth Street in the early 1900s. (Courtesy Florida State Archives.)

One hundred years after its founding, Joe's Stone Crab ranks as one of the top US restaurants in generating revenue, according to *Restaurant Business Magazine*. This world-famous restaurant began as a modest diner, as seen in this photograph from the early 1920s. It continues to attract an international clientele and is the go-to place if one visits Miami Beach. (Courtesy Florida State Archives.)

Rose Levy (on the left) and a friend are seated on a handmade horse between Second and Third Streets on Ocean Drive near Hardie's Casino in 1925, which was around the corner from Beth Jacob, located near the southern tip of Miami Beach. Hardie's Casino, the property of Dade County sheriff Dan Hardie, was a popular bathing casino for many attracted by the warm waters of the Atlantic Ocean. Bathing casinos offered food prepared on a grill, lockers, swimming pools, comfortable chairs for sun worshippers, and showers. (Courtesy Florida State Archives.)

Frank, Larry, and Herbie Glickman, early residents of Miami Beach, are posing for a picture on a beach in 1921. Underlining the "exotic" nature of the area was the propensity of families like the Glickmans as well as visitors to pose with stuffed alligators. (Courtesy Florida State Archives.)

From left to right, Herbert Glickman, Dennis Quittner, and Frank Glickman are standing on the beach in 1923. Until the beginning of the 1920s, the area of Miami Beach north of the bathing casinos in the south was undeveloped and underused as the community looked westward toward Biscayne Bay, with its rising hotels on the bayfront and its powerboat races and other thrilling spectacles. (Courtesy Florida State Archives.)

Arthur (left) and Jack (right) Courshon are pictured with a toy airplane in 1925. The Courshon brothers went on to become successful civic leaders and founders of the island's Jefferson National Bank and Washington Savings & Loan. Both served in the Army Air Corps in World War II as pilot and bombardier, respectively. (Courtesy Florida State Archives.)

From left to right, Bessie, Milton, and Isadore Gaynor are posing next to a palm tree in 1926. The close-knit Gaynor family is captured here in a "tourist pose," complete with the ubiquitous coconut palm tree and stuffed alligator. Milton's successful career in banking and other financial endeavors included his role in the founding of two Miami Beach banks. (Courtesy Florida State Archives.)

Bobby Iva (on the left) and Frank Glickman are pictured in a boxing ring in 1923. The young pugilists were carted around Miami Beach on a wagon upon which a boxing ring had been fitted as part of a carnival. (Courtesy Florida State Archives.)

Miami Beach is seen here near Fourteenth Street and Ocean Drive. From the 1920s into the early post–World War II era, Miami Beach's Lummus Park around Fourteenth Street was a popular gathering place for Jewish bathers, from school-age children to adults with families who enjoyed not only the warm waters of the Atlantic, but also picnicking or catching up on news from relatives and friends. (Courtesy of Miami-Dade Public Library, Romer Collection.)

Built in the 1920s, the Sea Breeze Hotel at 205 Collins Avenue was one of the beach's first kosher hotels. Billing itself as "The house of happiness," the hotel boasted of the "finest strictly kosher food served" as well as free entertainment. The blocks in the immediate vicinity of the hotel contained many Jewish families and represented the hub of the island's Jewish population. (Courtesy Larry Wiggins.)

Aaron (left) and Arthur (right) Courshon stand in Flamingo Park in 1928. Standing across from the famed Flamingo Hotel on the bayfront, Flamingo Park was the city's first park, a massive space in the southwest sector of Miami Beach. The park offers facilities for a wide variety of sports with large passive areas. Flamingo Park was, arguably, as popular as the beach less than one mile east of there. (Courtesy Florida State Archives.)

Lincoln Road was carved out of a mangrove jungle in the 1910s by Carl Fisher. Within two decades of its creation, Lincoln Road attracted many of Greater Miami's most posh national stores and offered cinemas, office buildings, and fine restaurants. By the 1950s, however, Lincoln Road was struggling, facing stiff retail competition from hotel-based stores and new shopping centers. City officials believed the solution was closing Lincoln Road to automotive traffic and bracketing it with lush shade trees. Morris Lapidus, the great architect of the Fontainebleau and Eden Roc, oversaw its conversion, with additions for rest and relaxation to its already built environment. While the "reinvented" Lincoln Road succeeded for a while, a few decades later the vendors again experienced financial problems. When the renaissance of the Art Deco area swept north/northwest in the 1990s, Lincoln Road was once more revived. Lapidus, now in his 90s, again applied his magic to the shopping street by adding many new and beautiful designs. (Courtesy of Miami-Dade Public Library, Romer Collection.)

This c. 1920s photograph shows the residence of Henri Levy, who developed the Normandy Isles and a portion of the town of Surfside. French-born Henri Levy; his wife, Rose Levy; and their children were said to be among the first Jewish families to move north of Miami Beach's Fifth Street, which had been the unofficial barrier between the island's Jewish and Gentile residents. In the 1920s, Washington Avenue, which stands in front of the house, was comprised of packed sand and flanked by towering Australian pine trees. For the Levys, the nearest house of worship was Beth Jacob, less than one mile south of them. (Courtesy Trevor Green.)

Normandy Isle Fountain at Intersection of Everglades Concourse and Normandy Drive, Miami Beach, Florida

Henry Levy's beautiful development on Normandy Isle was heralded by an eponymous fountain at its eastern entrance. Built in the 1920s, the fountain remains an integral part of a busy neighborhood featuring retail and restaurants. Beyond these elements are the residential components of Normandy Isle, with many streets bearing French names inspired by Levy's country of origin, France. (Courtesy Larry Wiggins.)

Pictured above is Miss Friedman's third-grade class at Miami Beach Elementary School, which was the island's first public elementary school, in 1927. Friedman (standing center, middle row) was the first Jewish teacher in the Miami Beach public school system. Among those students seen in this photograph are Jewish children from the Berkowitz, Kaplan, Ettinger, and Zinn families. (Courtesy Florida State Archives.)

Sol Goldstrom is standing in front of his Electrik Maid Bake Shop in the 1300 block of Washington Avenue around 1925. Washington Avenue served as a hub for Jewish businesses. Goldstrum's store was one of the first Jewish-owned businesses on the avenue. A half century later in the 1970s and 1980s, many Jewish businesses, from groceries to eateries, catered to the aging Jewish occupants of the hotels and apartments on South Beach. (Courtesy Florida State Archives.)

Leonard Abess was a financial wizard who arrived in Miami from New York at the crest of the great real estate boom of the mid-1920s. A certified public accountant, Abess entered into a business relationship as well as a deep friendship with Baron de Hirsch Meyer. Together, they founded a savings and loan bank on Miami Beach. Later, Abess was the moving force behind the creation and expansion of the large City National Bank institution as well as a major philanthropist to many institutions, especially Mount Sinai Medical Center. The institution's name was Mount Sinai Hospital until the 1970s, when it became Mount Sinai Medical Center, reflective of its enhanced physical plant and many new services. (Courtesy HistoryMiami Museum.)

The mighty hurricane of September 17–18, 1926, brought great destruction to Miami Beach. This image dramatizes the damage from the storm in South Beach. Many Jewish businesses and living quarters suffered significantly from the wrath of a storm carrying winds of more than 130 miles per hour. The hurricane left more than 130 persons dead and thousands homeless in the Greater Miami area. (Courtesy of Larry Wiggins.)

Two

DEPRESSION-ERA MIAMI BEACH

One of Henry Hohauser's masterpieces was the Cardozo Hotel, named for US Supreme Court justice Benjamin Cardozo, a Jew, who died in 1938, one year before the hotel's completion. In the late 1950s, the hostelry was the venue for Frank Sinatra's movie *A Hole in the Head*. Twenty years later, it was the first hotel to augur a turnaround in the fortunes of the newly anointed Art Deco District after Barbara Capitman, the district's champion, and her sons purchased the building and other nearby tarnished "jewels." The Capitmans opened a small bar in the Cardozo that drew an artistic clientele and set the stage for a slow turnaround of the longtime retiree haven into the world-famous resort and destination of today. (Courtesy of Miami-Dade Public Library, Romer Collection.)

FLORIDA   JAN. 1939

Hyman Galbut stands in front of Navy seaplanes in January 1939. A few years later, he was serving as a naval captain in World War II. (Courtesy Russell Galbut.)

June Levy, a gifted musician, is pictured here with her violin. A longtime Miami Beach resident, Levy played Kol Nidre, a Hebrew and Aramaic prayer before the beginning of the evening service on every Yom Kippur, the Day of Atonement. Levy was the daughter of Henri Levy, the creator of the Normandy Isles and a portion of today's Surfside. (Courtesy Florida State Archives.)

Members of the Levy and Huttenhaues families are seen here enjoying a picnic on South Beach in 1930. Behind them is the signature oolite limestone wall in Lummus Park, which still stands. A day at the beach was a highlight for the many working-class Jewish families who comprised most of the Jewish population of Miami Beach of that era. Many hailed from New York. (Courtesy Florida State Archives.)

Lloyd Ruskin, son of Mollie and Dan Ruskin, is seen here in the unlikely venue of a goat cart in Miami Beach in 1932. Dan was a highly successful entrepreneur and a partner with his brother-in-law Max Orovitz, a civic leader. Orovitz and Ruskin were active in a broad array of businesses, including natural gas, cement manufacturing, and home and community building. Lloyd, an attorney, served as vice chairman of the board of Fedco, a pharmaceutical chain. (Courtesy Florida State Archives.)

MIAMI·FLA.

1938·FEBRUARY·1938

The Edelstein family enjoyed the warm waters of Miami Beach, as seen in this image from 1938. From left to right are (first row) Harold; (second row) Mary and Morris; (third row) and Seymour. Miami Beach's Jewish community flocked to the northern portions of Lummus Park around Thirteenth and Fourteenth Streets and Ocean Drive, 10 blocks north of Beth Jacob, which was the preferred place to relax. (Courtesy Florida State Archives.)

Miami Beach residents Lilian and Matthew Silverstein, along with their daughters Abbey (left) and Irma (right), were captured spending a day at the beach. The family hailed from Brooklyn, moving to Miami Beach in 1935. The 1930s witnessed a significant increase in the number of Jewish denizens of Miami Beach, approaching 5,000 by the end of the decade. Irma later served as an Army nurse in World War II, and in the 1950s, she sat as a member of the Florida House of Representatives. (Courtesy Florida State Archives.)

Brothers Richard and Buddy Stone are seen here dressed for the "Pirates of Love" Valentine party in 1934. Nathan Stone with his wife, Lily, the boys' parents, built and operated the Blackstone Hotel, one of the first Jewish-owned hotels on Miami Beach and the tallest beach structure with 13 stories in 1929. This Mediterranean-style building at 830 Washington Avenue opened the same year as Beth Jacob and was just down the road. It was a favorite venue for Jews, many of whom had been turned away from other hotels because of anti-Semitism. (Courtesy Florida State Archives.)

Erected in 1938, the Park Central Hotel, looming over the southern portions of the Art Deco District, was a work that its designer, Henry Hohauser, was especially proud. The iconic structure was also a "game changer" in the fortunes of the Art Deco District when it caught the eye of preservationist and investor Tony Goldman, who made his fabled turn onto Ocean Drive from Fifth Street in the mid-1980s and knew instinctively he had to own it. Goldman had an impressive track record of restoring old buildings and neighborhoods in the Northeast, not only making them economically viable again, but also sparking a robust rebirth of the neighborhoods. He purchased and restored numerous buildings in the Art Deco District in the late 1980s and early 1990s, placing the district on the road to worldwide fame. (Courtesy of Miami-Dade Public Library, Romer Collection.)

Henry Hohauser also designed the Essex House Hotel at Collins Avenue and Tenth Street. This late-1930s Art Deco original, a short walk north from Beth Jacob, evokes the illusion of a ship's prow headed in the direction of the onlooker. Like other hotels in the Art Deco District, its fortunes declined sharply in the post–World War II era, as new, more elaborate hotels opened in Mid-Beach and beyond. By the late 1980s, with the fortunes of the Art Deco on fire with new investment and redevelopment, the Essex House Hotel underwent a complete restoration and soon became a stellar attraction in the constellation of Art Deco hotels in the neighborhood. (Courtesy of Miami-Dade Public Library, Romer Collection.)

Atlantic Ocean

Indian Creek

GENTILE CLIENTELE

Directions to

The Churchill HOTEL

From U. S. Highway No. 1 turn left at 79th Street
Causeway to ocean, then go south to 38th Street. See
Churchill Apartment Hotel.

From West Coast use County Causeway at 13th St. to
Collins Ave., turn left to 38th St. See Churchill Apt. Hotel.

The Churchill

ON BEAUTIFUL INDIAN CREEK • OVERLOOKING THE OCEAN
38th St. between Collins Ave. and Indian Creek Drive

M I A M I   B E A C H

"An Address of Distinction"
LOCATED IN THE EXCLUSIVE NORTH BEACH SECTION

An Art Deco hotel tracing its beginnings to the 1930s, the Churchill Hotel overlooked the languid waters of Indian Creek at Thirty-Eighth Street. Similar to other hotels on the beach, it boldly advertised itself as a hostelry for "Gentile Clientele" only or as "restricted." Only with a surging post–World War II Jewish population changing the ethnic composition of the beach and legislation forbidding gentleman's agreements and discrimination did these blatantly anti-Semitic restrictions come down by the mid-1950s. (Courtesy of Larry Wiggins.)

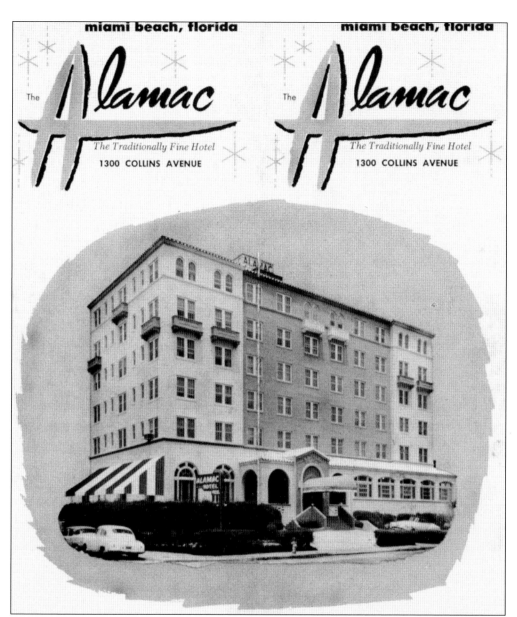

miami beach, florida   miami beach, florida

The *Alamac*

The *Alamac*

The Traditionally Fine Hotel

1300 COLLINS AVENUE

The Traditionally Fine Hotel

1300 COLLINS AVENUE

An early Jewish-owned hotel on Miami Beach, the Alamac still stands at 1300 Collins Avenue, a short walk north from Beth Jacob. Built at the onset of the 1930s, the hostelry was operated in its early years by the Rosenthal family. The Alamac offered guests a strictly kosher cuisine, a grand swimming pool, and large solariums. It was one of pre–World War II Miami Beach's tallest hotels. It is now an apartment community. (Courtesy of Larry Wiggins.)

The Lord Balfour Hotel at 350 Ocean Drive was designed in 1940 by Anton Skislewicz, a European architect, for Morris Zarrow. The architect admired Lord Balfour and his call for a Jewish homeland and named the hotel to honor the British foreign secretary. The Balfour Declaration of 1917 supported the establishment of a Jewish homeland in Ottoman-controlled Palestine. (Courtesy of Larry Wiggins.)

The Betsy Ross Hotel, today's Betsy, on Ocean Drive and Fourteenth Lane was atypical of the hotels built on Ocean Drive in the late 1930s. Designed by famed architect L. Murray Dixon, it was neo-Colonial in contrast to the Streamline Moderne or Art Deco style of other hotels in that area. In its early years of operation, the hotel was operated by Sol Schimmel, managing director. (Courtesy of Larry Wiggins.)

Mr. and Mrs. Louis Miller, owners of the storied Victor Hotel on Ocean Drive and Thirteenth Street, are seated in the hotel's dining room in 1941. Designed by famed architect L. Murray Dixon and built in 1937, the Victor was one of the tallest Art Deco hotels of that era. Louis Miller is emblematic of the growing presence of Jewish builders who brought the Streamline Moderne (Art Deco) style to South Beach in the 1930s. (Courtesy Florida State Archives.)

Leonard Wein's achievements as a developer were on display at Collins Avenue and Eleventh Street where three Art Deco jewels arose in the second half of the 1930s, all walking distance to Beth Jacob. The Tudor Hotel is seen here. Designed by L. Murray Dixon, it highlighted decorative finials. (Courtesy of Larry Wiggins.)

Developer Morris Ginsburg constructed the Mercantile Bank Building, seen here on the far left side of this image. Standing at the bustling intersection of Lincoln Road and Washington Avenue, the Mercantile Bank Building towered over Lincoln Road. Its ground floor contained the eponymous bank, retail stores, and the Beach Theater. The offices above included those of the S&G gambling syndicate, comprised of five Jewish entrepreneurs who controlled the lucrative gambling operations on Miami Beach in the 1940s. (Courtesy of Larry Wiggins.)

Isadore and Florence Hecht, an early Miami Beach "power couple," were new residents of the island at the time of this photograph, taken around 1940. Married in 1938, the Hechts moved to Miami Beach the following year from Boston. They played an active role in many sectors of the community's business, civic, and religious life. In the 1950s, the Hechts bought the West Flagler Dog Track in Miami, which was a popular South Florida destination for both locals and visitors until the turn of the century. (Courtesy Florida State Archives.)

The photograph above is of Russian immigrant Abraham "Al" Galbut's store and newsstand at Fifth Street and Washington Avenue on Miami Beach in 1938. Galbut transformed the establishment from a newsstand, with papers in Yiddish and English, in the early 1930s to a bustling all-night luncheonette in the 1940s that local politicians, military men, and the city's dignitaries would frequent. Seen in the photograph are Hyman (far left, age 18) and his father, Al (second from left). The others are unidentified. The photograph below, taken in 1938, is of the interior of the store, which also served as the first Driver's Tag Agency on the beach. (Both, courtesy Russell Galbut.)

Three generations of the Dermers are seen here on a winter vacation on Miami Beach in 1939. Son Jay, second from right, moved to Miami Beach from the Northeast in 1955 as a newly minted attorney before running for political office in the following decade. In 1967, Dermer defeated incumbent mayor Elliot Roosevelt, son of Pres. Franklin D. Roosevelt, in his inaugural bid for political office. While mayor, Dermer campaigned for beach renourishment and the opening of all beaches to the public and opposed casino gambling, which was a hot button issue in the resort city of that era and beyond. Dermer served two terms before leaving office in 1971. (Courtesy Florida State Archives.)

Seen here are members of Miami Beach Boy Scout Troop 33 in 1932. Miami Beach was a superb home for Scouts—compact and neighborly and surrounded by warm waters and subtropical foliage. It lent itself to awesome nature experiences. Many Jewish youths were members of this troop. (Courtesy Florida State Archives.)

Founded in 1927 near the southern tip of Miami Beach, Beth Jacob is Miami Beach's oldest Jewish congregation. The building on the left opened its door for services in 1929. Next to it is the 1936 Art Deco synagogue, an architectural gem designed by Beth Jacob member Henry Hohauser, one of Miami Beach's preeminent Art Deco architects. Today, the complex hosts the Jewish Museum of Florida. (Courtesy HistoryMiami Museum.)

Bill Baros with a Committee
of Jewish War Veterans
presenting the American Fla,
at the Dedication Ceremonie
of the Miami Beach Jewish
                    Cent
                    9/1.

Bill Baros (center) is saluting the flag accompanied by a committee of veterans of the armed forces. The occasion is the dedication of the Miami Beach Jewish Community Center in September 1941. Three months after the dedication, the nation was at war following the Japanese aerial attack on Pearl Harbor. The center bore numerous names in its early years before becoming Temple Emanu-El (which is Hebrew for "God be with Us") in 1954. (Courtesy Florida State Archives.)

Three

WARTIME MIAMI BEACH

A Passover seder at Temple Beth Jacob's Servicemen's Center was sponsored by the Jewish Welfare Board in 1943. The synagogue provided a gathering place for many Jewish servicemen during World War II. Beth Jacob was the first beach synagogue to invite local residents and visitors in the area to its synagogue to celebrate Jewish holidays. (Courtesy Florida State Archives.)

Seen in this wartime photograph is Navy captain Hyman Galbut. He arrived in Miami Beach with his family at the age of seven in 1927, the year after the devastating 1926 hurricane. Galbut attended Miami Beach Senior High and later opened a law firm on the beach while continuing to serve, after the war, in the Navy Reserve, rallying recruits. (Courtesy Russell Galbut.)

Baron de Hirsch Meyer served in the armed forces, as seen in this image taken in 1942. While not a baron, de Hirsch Meyer was a very successful businessman, especially in the field of banking. Armed with a law degree from Harvard University, de Hirsch Meyer amassed great wealth and with his wife, the beautiful former showgirl and developer Polly Lux de Hirsch Meyer, gave away millions to such institutions as Mount Sinai Medical Center and the Miami Jewish Home and Hospital for the Aged. Baron also made a splash in politics, becoming the first Jew elected to the Miami Beach City Council in 1930. (Courtesy Florida State Archives.)

Marjorie Wein is seen here in her American Red Cross uniform during World War II in the early 1940s. Wein and her husband, Leonard, moved to Miami from New York in 1935. Soon after, Leonard began building beautiful Art Deco/Streamline Moderne hotels along Collins Avenue, including the Tudor, Palmer House, and Kent, each side by side on the 1100 block. Leonard was also a prolific home builder, accounting for the construction of more than 1,000 homes throughout fast-growing Dade County. Marjorie and Leonard were leaders in the Jewish community and among the founders of Miami Beach's Mount Sinai Hospital. Marjorie founded the Godmothers of Mount Sinai and raised monies for a maternity wing. The institution's Wien Center for Alzheimer's Disease and Memory Disorders is named for them. (Courtesy Florida State Archives.)

Gray Ladies of Nautilus Hospital posed for this group photograph in 1944. With America's entrance into World War II, several of the area hotels were converted to military hospitals. Opened in 1924 by Carl Fisher, the Nautilus Hotel on Miami Beach, a Mediterranean-style jewel, was among those hotels converted to hospitals. The Gray Ladies of the Nautilus Hospital were Red Cross volunteers with representation throughout the United States in World War I and World War II. They provided friendly, personal, nonmedical services to patients in need of care. Their assistance extended to writing letters, reading, tutoring, and shopping for patients. The Nautilus was "surplussed" by the federal government after the war and, in 1949, became the new home of Mount Sinai Hospital. (Courtesy Florida State Archives.)

Temple Beth Jacob rabbi Moses Mescheloff (first row, left) of New York presents a Sefer Torah (the five books of Moses, the Pentateuch) to members of the Army Air Corps in 1944. Thousands of Jewish Army Air Force trainees populated Miami Beach between 1942 and 1945 and prayed at Beth Jacob. Rabbi Mescheloff was generous with his time with Jewish troops and provided guidance to those observing their traditions in their new, temporary home. (Courtesy Florida State Archives.)

A Passover seder drew many attendees to the recently created Miami Beach Jewish Community Center in 1942. Among those in attendance at the beginning of the Jewish holiday of Passover were members of the Army Air Force who were training on Miami Beach. The seder, a ceremonial dinner, is based on the Torah verses commanding Jews to retell the story of their exodus from Egypt annually. (Courtesy Florida State Archives.)

The Miami Beach Jewish Community Center attracted large numbers of Jewish servicemen training with the Army Air Force on Miami Beach during World War II. Besides offering them a place to worship, the center provided entertainment, food, and even temporary housing. Particularly helpful was "Mother" Bloom, a member of the congregation, and her committee who cooked, baked, and distributed food to hungry GIs throughout the war years. She and her committee spent each day and part of the evening serving the nutritional needs of "her" military clientele. This photograph was taken in 1943. (Courtesy Florida State Archives.)

Lenny Koos (left) and Jerry Jacobs (right) are shown here at the time of their liberation from a Nazi prison in Saint-Valery, France, in 1944. Jacobs was a fighter pilot who was shot down over Germany and taken prisoner for nine months in 1944. Liberated by Allied forces under the command of US general George C. Patton, Jacobs became a dentist, moved to Miami Beach from Philadelphia in 1953, and authored *Some Came Home* about his experiences in the Army Air Forces in World War II. (Courtesy Florida State Archives.)

Built in 1935, the Hotel Evans, as it was then known, was a sprawling Mediterranean-style complex that graces the bustling intersection of Collins Avenue and Tenth Street. Isadore Evans and family, who operated the Evans hotel in the Catskills, moved to the beach to provide lodging for Jews who were restricted by "Gentile Only" signs. When the Army Air Corps leased Miami Beach hotels and restaurants in World War II, the Hotel Evans, with its grand banquet room and central location, was a popular mess hall for feeding large numbers of soldiers daily and served as barracks with its 150 hotel rooms. In September 1944, the Army returned the facility to its owners to again be operated as a hotel. (Courtesy of Myron Davis.)

A VE (Victory in Europe) Day breakfast was provided by a chapter of Aleph Zadik Aleph, a B'nai B'rith youth group affiliated with the Miami Beach Jewish Community Center. May 8, 1945, brought both jubilance and sorrow on Miami Beach and in Jewish communities everywhere as news of Germany's surrender in Europe was juxtaposed with the revelations of the horrors of Nazi death camps. (Courtesy Florida State Archives.)

This aerial view captures the lush grounds and picturesque buildings comprising the Nautilus Hotel. The hotel was designed by Schultze and Weaver, a stellar New York architectural firm, and built in 1924 by Carl Fisher, the "founder" of Miami Beach and an anti-Semite. After serving as a military hospital in World War II, the hotel became the home of Mount Sinai Hospital in 1949. Mount Sinai was created just a few years earlier in part to provide opportunities for young Jewish physicians who experienced discrimination from many hospitals in their quest for residencies. In the 1970s, the expanding hospital and medical complex now called itself Mount Sinai Medical Center. (Courtesy of Miami-Dade Public Library, Romer Collection.)

Gershon's News Stand at Dade Pharmacy on busy Fifth Street in South Beach, less than a five-minute walk from Beth Jacob, was a must visit for residents and visitors thirsting for news. The newsstand's selection of out-of-town newspapers was second to none in the area. This was especially so for Jewish patrons from New York and other northeastern cities. (Courtesy of Miami-Dade Public Library, Romer Collection.)

Wolfie's Restaurant on Collins Avenue and Twenty-First Street was the beach's most famous kosher eatery from its opening in 1943 until the waning years of the 20th century. Open 24 hours, its popularity led to the opening of a second Wolfie's on Collins Avenue and Lincoln Road. Wolfie Cohen, its owner and proprietor, offered crowds of visitors and local residents oversized hot pastrami sandwiches with free pickles and coleslaw. (Courtesy of Miami-Dade Public Library, Romer Collection.)

Rabbi Irving Lehrman had been the spiritual leader of the Miami Beach Jewish Community Center for three years when he and his wife, Belle, were honored at a dinner in 1946. The couple is seated at the center of the photograph. Three years earlier, the young rabbi was installed as the new spiritual leader of the Miami Beach Jewish Community Center, today's Temple Emanu-El. Over the next five decades, Rabbi Lehrman's vibrant personality and powerful sermons transformed the small congregation into one of the most prominent conservative synagogues in America. A larger-than-life spiritual leader, he participated in many organizations locally, nationally, and internationally. (Courtesy Florida State Archives.)

In Jewish tradition, the holiday sukkah is Biblical and celebrated shortly after the Day of Atonement (Yom Kippur). In this photograph is a sukkah breakfast in 1943 at the Miami Beach Jewish Community Center. Located on Euclid Avenue at Fourteenth Place, the center grew quickly and was soon offering a wide array of activities and events that catered to South Beach Jewish residents. (Courtesy Florida State Archives.)

A Miami Beach Jewish Community Center (renamed Temple Emanu-El) youth basketball team posed for this photograph in 1943. Many of its youth groups and institutions were already beginning to grow legs and establish robust programs. In the postwar years, members of the youth basketball team attended Miami Beach High School with its large population of Jewish students, and the school became one of the basketball powers of the area. (Courtesy Florida State Archives.)

Miami Beach High School senior prom was held in 1942, shortly after the nation entered World War II. The school traces its origins to 1927 when it was known as Ida M. Fisher High School. Until the early 1960s, the school (now a middle school) stood in the heart of South Beach at Fourteenth Street and Drexel Avenue, one mile north of Beth Jacob. Many of its Jewish graduates enlisted in the armed forces in World War II. The hotels and apartments near the school were filled with Army Air Force trainees. In the courtyard of the school stand statues of soldiers provided by the graduation classes following the war's end and placed there in honor of those earlier graduates who gave their lives for their country and the Allied war cause. (Courtesy Florida State Archives.)

Irving Frankel, campaign chairperson for the hotel division of the Greater Miami Jewish Federation, is pictured at a fundraiser on Miami Beach in the early 1940s. The federation supports many activities of the Miami-Dade Jewish community, especially those in need. (Courtesy Florida State Archives.)

Built in 1936, Congregation Beth Jacob's second house of worship includes a stained glass window purchased by gangster Meyer Lansky, who attended services there during Yom Kippur (Day of Atonement) and lived on Miami Beach. Lansky's window is impaneled in the central portion of the building's south wall, seen here. Today, the building is home to the Jewish Museum of Florida-FIU. (Courtesy of Larry Wiggins.)

Four

MID-CENTURY
MIAMI BEACH

An exuberant Miriam Feit and Saul Rose walk together as husband and wife toward the entrance of Beth Jacob, which highlighted, in 1948, the newly refurbished sanctuary of the Art Deco–style Beth Jacob synagogue. This synagogue was designed in the mid-1930s by renowned architect Henry Hohauser, who was a member of Beth Jacob and lived nearby. (Courtesy Florida State Archives.)

Shortly after the founding of Temple Beth Sholom in the early 1940s, a religious school was established. The Temple Beth Sholom Religious School has maintained a rigor in its approach to learning, and many of the enrollees have gone on to successful careers in a wide array of endeavors, among them Robert Rubin, secretary of the US Treasury during the Clinton presidency. The school was already a core foundational attraction for the growing Jewish population of the beach in the late 1940s and 1950s. (Courtesy Temple Beth Sholom.)

The photograph above is a portrait of the Galbut family in the backyard of their home on Royal Palm Avenue in Miami Beach around the 1950s. Pictured are, from left to right, (first row) sons Robert, Al B. (on David's lap), Russell (on Bessie's lap), and Hyman; (second row) David and his wife, Bessie; (third row) David's mother, Bessie. Members of the Galbut family have been prominent benefactors of the Beth Jacob synagogue as well as the greater Jewish community in Miami Beach. (Courtesy Russell Galbut.)

Sisterhood, which dates to the inception of Temple Beth Sholom (which in Hebrew means "House of Peace"), represents one of the earliest, strongest, and most enduring features of Temple Beth Sholom's committees. Members of Sisterhood are seen here preparing for a musical presentation in the early 1950s. Their presentations were enthusiastically embraced by members of the congregation. (Courtesy Temple Beth Sholom.)

Grace and Henry Hohauser are pictured here in 1950. Henry Hohauser, a New Yorker educated at the Pratt Institute in Brooklyn, arrived in Miami Beach during the early years of the Depression and was one of the island's most prolific and celebrated Art Deco architects. Among the more than 100 buildings Hohauser designed in the 1930s and 1940s are the dazzling Park Central, Colony, Carlton, Essex House, and Cardozo Hotels. (Courtesy Florida State Archives.)

Kenneth and Helyne Triester, who were married in 1954, are seen here in their wedding portrait. A graduate of Miami Beach High School, Ken Triester is a nationally and internationally renowned architect for his award-winning design of commercial, residential, institutional, and public buildings, including the Holocaust Memorial on Miami Beach, the Mayfair Shops and Hotel in Coconut Grove, and the ethereal Gumenick Chapel on Temple Israel's campus north of downtown Miami. (Courtesy Florida State Archives.)

Nathan and Lillian Silverman are pictured here in the Bon Aire Motel bar in 1956. The Silvermans owned this "Motel Row" hotel in today's Sunny Isles Beach, north of Northeast 163rd Street along Collins Avenue, in the extreme northern environs of Dade County. This glitzy portion of the beach exploded in growth following World War II with snowbirds capitalizing on real estate opportunities. The motels were designed in exotic ways and highlighted the emerging Miami Modern or Mid-Century Miami style of design, featuring curvilinear shapes, extensive balconies, and plenty of glass. Today, these hospitality lodgings have been replaced by towering, expensive condominiums with many former Soviet Jews and French-speaking Jews from France and Montreal as residents. (Courtesy Florida State Archives.)

Sammy Davis Jr., as seen at a table in Miami Beach's Raleigh Hotel surrounded by adoring fans, was one of America's finest entertainers in the middle decades of the 20th century. He performed on Miami Beach, sometimes with Frank Sinatra and other members of the Rat Pack at the capacious Fontainebleau. A Jew through conversion, he found commonalities between the oppression experienced by Black Americans and members of the Jewish community. Davis was among the first Black entertainers to perform on the beach. (Courtesy Charles Carlini.)

Rabbi Mayer Abramowitz, seen here in this early-2000s photograph with Norma Orovitz, the first woman president of Miami's Temple Israel, lived a highly eventful and meaningful life long before becoming the rabbi of Temple Menorah in the early 1950s. Abramowitz served this North Beach congregation as its rabbi for 45 years. In earlier times, he assisted thousands of refugees who survived World War II in making aliyah (immigration) to Palestine, and later Cuban Jews in the 1960s who migrated to Miami Beach. (Courtesy Norma Orovitz.)

Samuel Beckerman (seated, left), vice president of Temple Beth Sholom, is shown presenting a $2,500 State of Israel Bond to Rabbi Kronish (seated, right) on behalf of the congregation. Rabbi Kronish was instrumental in launching the State of Israel Bond drives to support Israel's fledgling economy in 1951 and was one of America's most important Zionist rabbis in the second half of the 20th century. With Beckerman and Kronish are Abraham Zinnamon (standing, left), treasurer, and Shepard Broad (standing, right), president of the congregation in early 1950s. (Courtesy Temple Beth Sholom.)

This late-1940s photograph showcases the construction of a new house of worship for the Miami Beach Jewish Community Center (renamed Temple Emanu-El in 1954). Designed by architect Charles Greco and modeled after the Great Synagogue in Algiers, Algeria, it was the largest synagogue in the southern United States (1,800 worshippers) when it opened in 1948. The synagogue was highlighted by a Byzantine copper dome and a sanctuary free of columns, so that no worshipper's vision would be impaired. (Courtesy Florida State Archives.)

Seen in the photograph above is architect Percival Goodman's early-1950s rendering of a new home for Temple Beth Sholom. His daring design seen here depicts, in the description of other designers, a "shell emerging from the ground, embracing the bimah and bathing it with colored light from an array of parabolic vaults." The sculptural mass of Goodman's sanctuary design remains the core of the campus after nearly seven decades. (Courtesy of Larry Wiggins.)

Shephard Broad (right) was a Russian immigrant and orphan who arrived in the United States by way of Canada in 1920 at age 14. Andrew Stark, pictured here on Broad's left, rescued him from the ship carrying him to North America. After practicing law in New York, Broad visited the Florida Keys on a fishing trip in 1939, fell in love with the area, and moved to Miami Beach. (Courtesy Florida State Archives.)

Morris Edelstein (right), an early Jewish resident of Miami Beach, is seen here in his World War I US Navy uniform. Next to him is his son Seymour wearing his World War II Army uniform. Both men were proud of their service and patriotism to their country and to the freedoms it provided its citizenry. (Courtesy Florida State Archives.)

A conference of Jewish women's organizations of Dade and Broward Counties took place on Miami Beach in 1954. Pictured are, from left to right, (first row) Matilda Ratner, Mrs. Aaron Farr, Mrs. Milton Sirkin, and Mrs. A. Frank Wellins; (second row) Mrs. Benjamin Appel, Mrs. Irwin Wenstein, Mrs. Julian Weindle, Mrs. Harry Rogers, Mrs. Monte Selig, and Mrs. Irving Lehrson. By the mid-1970s, Greater Miami's Jewish population peaked at over 275,000 with Miami Beach at the core. (Courtesy Florida State Archives.)

Three generations of the pioneering Weiss family gathered for this photograph at the family-owned Royal Apartments in 1949. From left to right are (first row) Hannah Sayetta holding Kay (Weiss) Harris; (second row) Rose and Eugene Weiss. The Royal Apartments stood near the southern tip of Miami Beach and were among the first Jewish-owned buildings on the island, a stone's throw from Beth Jacob. Rose Weiss was called the "Mother of Miami Beach" for her contributions to the city's development. (Courtesy Florida State Archives.)

Wolfie's opened immediately after the conclusion of World War II at 1 Lincoln Road on Miami Beach. The restaurant and sandwich shop drew large local and tourist crowds each and every night, which followed the business's slogan that "When you come to Miami Beach, you must eat at Wolfie's." (Courtesy Larry Wiggins.)

During the mid-20th century, Collins Avenue in North Beach saw the opening of new hotels and restaurants. Wolfie Cohen's Pumperniks, located at Collins Avenue and Sixty-Seventh Street, quickly became a popular Jewish deli restaurant, bragging that it was the "Home of the Pumpernickel Bagel that Arthur Godfrey made famous." Godfrey was a famed radio and television personality who broadcast many of his shows in mid-century America from sunny Miami Beach. (Courtesy of Larry Wiggins.)

The cover of a lavish c. 1950 program for the offerings at Lou Walters's Latin Quarter is shown at left. By then, Lou Walters was operating two Latin Quarters: the club at Broadway and Forty-Eighth Street in New York City's Times Square and the Miami Beach edition on Palm Island in Biscayne Bay. These entertainment havens were among the most famous of this genre, drawing as guests America's entertainment royalty as well as an upscale crowd of other, not-so-famous patrons. Below, Walters's fabled Latin Quarter met an inglorious demise in 1959 when a fire destroyed the Art Deco-style building occupying the space of the earlier Palm Island Club, which had provided lavish entertainment for thousands of guests since its opening in 1939. Today, beautiful Island Park occupies the site of the posh club of yesteryear. (Both, courtesy of Larry Wiggins.)

Miami Beach Auditorium, an Art Deco gem, known today as the Fillmore at the Jackie Gleason Theater of the Performing Arts, was built at the outset of the 1950s. The building has hosted a dizzying variety of events and performances, including Frank Sinatra, Bob Hope, and Jack Benny, and served as a filming location for the *Ed Sullivan Show*, the *Dick Clark Show*, and the Miss USA Pageant. For six years, it was the home of *The Jackie Gleason Show*. For many years, it also housed the spillover of worshippers from nearby Temple Emanu-El during Passover and Yom Kippur. (Courtesy of Miami-Dade Public Library, Romer Collection.)

The Robert Richter Hotel arose along crowded Collins Avenue at Thirty-Third Street after World War II. Noted for its signature tower atop penthouse suites, the hotel branded itself the "Aristocrat of Miami Beach." The hotel was named for a son of the Richter family, Greater Miami's preeminent jeweler with a major presence in downtown Miami. Robert Richter was killed in combat in World War II. (Courtesy of Larry Wiggins.)

The Kenilworth Bal Harbour at Collins Avenue and 102nd Street was an early post–World War II hotel in Bal Harbour Village. Adjoining the hotel on its northern flank was the Kenilworth House, featuring suites with complete kitchen facilities and multiple bedroom arrangements, 400 feet of private beach, and two complete cabana areas. The hotel was "restricted," which meant it was off limits for Jews. One of its owners, television personality Arthur Godfrey, often recorded his show from there. (Courtesy of Larry Wiggins.)

SAN SOUCCI – MIAMI BEACH

In the bustling years following the conclusion of World War II, new luxury hotels opened along Collins Avenue, which became America's most famous tourist thoroughfare. The Sans Souci was one of the most spectacular. An exemplar of the early postwar Modern style, its architects were Roy France and Morris Lapidus. Standing between Thirty-First and Thirty-Second Streets, it is known today as the Riu Hotel. (Courtesy of Larry Wiggins.)

Romanian-born B. Robert Swartburg was a master of the post–World War II Mid-Century Modern style of architecture. Raised in New York City and a graduate of Columbia University, Swartburg migrated to Miami Beach during the real estate boom of the mid-1920s, stayed until 1928, and returned in 1944 to spend the remainder of his life. One of Swartburg's most important designs on Miami Beach was the Delano Hotel for Rob and Rose Schwartz, as seen on this postcard. (Courtesy Larry Wiggins.)

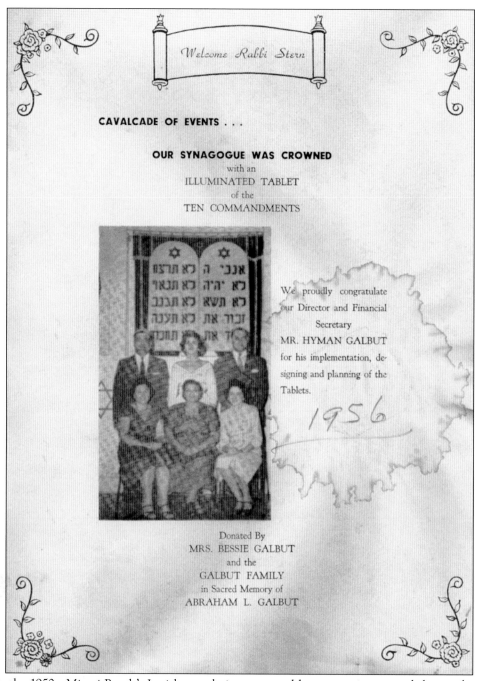

CAVALCADE OF EVENTS . . .

OUR SYNAGOGUE WAS CROWNED
with an
ILLUMINATED TABLET
of the
TEN COMMANDMENTS

אנכי ה׳ לא תרצח
לא יהיה לא תנאף
לא תשא לא תגנב
זכור את לא תענה
כבד את לא תחמד

We proudly congratulate our Director and Financial Secretary MR. HYMAN GALBUT for his implementation, designing and planning of the Tablets.

1956

Donated By
MRS. BESSIE GALBUT
and the
GALBUT FAMILY
in Sacred Memory of
ABRAHAM L. GALBUT

By the 1950s, Miami Beach's Jewish population grew and began moving toward the northern quarter of the city, while the Galbut family continued to nurture Beth Jacob and South Beach as a center for worship and education. In honor of the memory of Abraham Galbut's passing, the family donated an illuminated tablet of the Ten Commandments in 1956, as commemorated in the pamphlet above. Family members in attendance for the ceremony and seen in the picture on the January 6, 1956, program included, from left to right, (first row) Ethel, Bessie (Abraham's wife), and Bessie (Hyman's wife); (second row) Paul, Miriam, and Hyman. (Courtesy Russell Galbut.)

Five

A BEACH IN TRANSITION

Seen here in 1976 are Jewish residents of South Beach hotels enjoying the ambiance of Lummus Park and the ocean just beyond. By the 1970s, the world-famous Art Deco hotels of today were housing an elderly Jewish population who migrated to Miami Beach from the Northeast United States to enjoy their golden years. (Courtesy of HistoryMiami Museum.)

The above photograph shows the Galbut family outside the Beth Jacob synagogue during Robert Galbut's bar mitzvah in 1960. Robert's father, Hyman, also had his bar mitzvah at Beth Jacob in 1933 and later would serve as its president. Robert is standing in the center of the photograph with his parents, Hyman and Bessie, behind him. (Courtesy of Russell Galbut.)

Pictured is the storefront window of the Galbut & Galbut law office on Fifth Street and Washington Avenue in Miami Beach in 1964. Sensitive to the changing needs of the South Beach community, the law firm took on pro bono work for rudderless retirees and also represented real estate developers during the beach's boom years. (Courtesy of Russell Galbut.)

In the photograph above, several prominent Jewish leaders have gathered in Miami Beach. The men seen here, representing building, banking, finance, retail, and civic contributions to their Miami Beach community, gathered for this rare photograph in the 1960s. From left to right are (first row) Sam Blank, Dan Ruskin, Arthur Unger, and Joe Stein; (second row) Leonard Wein, Jack Albin, Dr. Morris Goodman, Bill Singer, and a Mr. Sher. (Courtesy Florida State Archives.)

Pictured here with US senator Hubert Humphrey in this 1963 photograph is Milton Gaynor (left), a successful banker and businessman who was a major force in Florida's Democratic Party. In 1964, Humphrey was elected vice president while Gaynor's resume continued to grow to include additional institutional and charitable involvements. (Courtesy Florida State Archives.)

Temple Beth Sholom Religious School students were in the forefront of the consecration ceremonies of the new Community House in December 1961 on Chase Avenue off Forty-First Street. In the background is the synagogue, built in 1953. Among the people are children of Beth Jacob's members. (Courtesy Temple Beth Sholom.)

Judy (Nelson) Drucker was a cultural impresario par excellence. A Miami Beach resident since 1941 and a musical prodigy with a mastery over many genres of music, Drucker, at the behest of Rabbi Leon Kronish, introduced in 1967 the Great Artists Series at Temple Beth Sholom. By the 1980s, Drucker expanded the cultural series, which, a few years later, segued into the award-winning Culture Association of Florida (CAF). As director of the CAF, Drucker became internationally acclaimed. She brought the world's greatest classical music orchestras, conductors, soloists, opera stars, and ballet and dance companies to town. (Courtesy Temple Beth Sholom.)

Some of Miami Beach's most prominent Jewish leaders are shown at a Mount Sinai Hospital Jubilee Ball in the late 1960s. Seen in the receiving line are Leonard Wein (second from left), Baron de Hirsch Meyer (fourth from left), and Max Orovitz (eighth from left). (Courtesy of Michael and Norma Orovitz.)

Taking a lunch break from the duties of governing the city, four city councilmen are seen fishing off a pier just south of Fifth Street on Miami Beach in 1963. South Beach is a water mecca not only for tourists, but also for lifelong residents and local leaders. Pictured are, from left to right, Hyman Galbut, Robert Turchin, Bernie Frank, and Mayor Mel Richard. (Courtesy of Russell Galbut.)

Judge Herbert S. Shapiro, shown around 1970, was a longtime resident of Miami Beach. He was the community's first Jewish administrative judge. The administrative judge court was located in Miami Beach's second city hall on Washington Avenue, near Eleventh Street. (Courtesy Florida State Archives.)

The affable Leonard Miller of Lennar Homes, one of Temple Beth Sholom's great lay leaders, is seen here flanked by Rabbi Kronish and Golda Meir during the Israeli prime minister's visit to Miami Beach in 1973. Temple Beth Sholom played a significant role when Israeli dignitaries came to Florida. (Courtesy Temple Beth Sholom.)

Maribel G. Blum cuts the ribbon on the new pavilion named for her, which houses the medical center radiation oncology division. Attending this ceremony in 1973 are, from left to right, Edward Shapiro, president, Mount Sinai Medical Center; Mildred Pepper; Congressman Claude Pepper; Rabbi Irving Lehrman of Temple Emanu-El; Max Orovitz, chairman of the board of trustees; Col. Jacob Avery; Samuel Gertner, executive director; Maribel Blum; Arnold Winnick; and Samuel Friedland, vice chairman of the board of trustees. (Courtesy of Michael and Norma Orovitz.)

Gathered in this photograph are members of the Deed (as in "Good Deed") Club, an active charitable organization assisting children with cancer. In the second half of the 20th century, this Miami Beach organization staged an annual musical production to help fund their Children's Cancer Clinic. This image captured the group in 1975 gathered for their 27th annual showtime production, *Puttin on the Ritz*, at the posh Fontainebleau Hotel. (Courtesy Florida State Archives.)

97

Lily Stone is shown assisting at the Miami Beach Hebrew House for the Aged at 310 Collins Avenue, immediately east of Beth Jacob, in 1978. By the late 1970s, South Beach was comprised mostly of elderly Jews, many from the Northeast United States who had moved south to spend their golden years in the sun. (Courtesy Florida State Archives.)

THE ARTIST'S DREAM

The Artist's Dream mural hung in the cocktail lounge of Lou Walters's spectacular Latin Quarter club on Palm Island in Miami Beach. Walters, a famed nightclub impresario, featured beautiful, costumed showgirls engaged in spectacular, carefully planned acts and shows, often swinging above the gathered crowd seated at tables below. Walters's daughter Barbara would achieve fame as an elite television commentator and personality. (Courtesy of Larry Wiggins.)

Pictured with University of Miami president Henry King Stanford (left), former US president Gerald Ford (second from right), and Clifford S. Perlman (right) at the University of Miami Athletic Scholarship Roast in February 1978, Rocky Pomerance (second from the left) was a large, jovial policeman who served as chief of the City of Miami Beach Police Department in the 1960s and 1970s. A New Yorker who moved to Miami Beach in 1950, Pomerance joined the city's police force in the 1950s and is best known for his effectiveness in keeping Miami Beach from falling into chaos during the Democratic and Republican presidential nominating conventions of 1972. The plaza in front of the Miami Beach Police Headquarters is named for him. (Courtesy of University of Miami.)

This is a photograph of Larry King, a radio host for Miami's WIOD in the early 1970s, during one of his broadcasts. He is interviewing three leaders of the area's Jewish community at the West Flagler Dog Track. From left to right are Leonard Abess, Isadore Hecht, Max Orovitz, and King. Larry King (born Lawrence Harvey Zeiger) left South Florida by the end of the 1970s and later gained fame on CNN by hosting the *Larry King Live* talk show, which became the channel's longest-running program between 1985 and 2010. (Courtesy Florida State Archives.)

The Orovitzs married and lived in Miami's Shenandoah neighborhood from the late 1920s through the early post–World War II years before moving to Miami Beach. As president of the Greater Miami Jewish Federation, Max traveled to Palestine in 1948 to bring needed resources. Ruth and Max Orovitz (seated at center) are surrounded by their children and their spouses and grandchildren. (Courtesy of Michael and Norma Orovitz.)

Sophia and Nathan Gumenick are pictured at Miami Beach's Southgate Towers, built by Nathan Gumenick, around the 1970s. Nathan was a prominent builder of apartment complexes in Virginia and Miami Beach and, together with his wife, Sophia, was a generous philanthropist to many causes, including Mount Sinai Medical Center, Temple Israel in Miami, and the Miami Jewish Home and Hospital for the Aged. (Courtesy Florida State Archives.)

Seen in the photograph above is Temple Beth Shmuel, the Cuban-Hebrew Congregation. The first stirrings for this conservative Ashkenazi congregation came in 1961 with the formation by 13 Cuban refugees of the Cuban Hebrew Circle of Miami. As the congregation grew, it changed its name to the Cuban-Hebrew Congregation. Inaugurated in 1984, Temple Beth Shmuel was home to waves of refugees from Cuba, including those from the Mariel boatlift. (Courtesy Trevor Green.)

Bernardo Benes, seen here with journalist, institutional, and civic leader Norma Orovitz, was a Cuban Jew who fled the island for Miami in 1960 to begin a new life in America after his father's company was expropriated by the Castro government. Benes, an attorney, worked as a banker and was a major figure in the Cuban exile community. He helped Operacion Pedro Pan children leave Cuba and advocated for the release of large numbers of political prisoners incarcerated in Cuba in the late 1970s. Bernardo Benes was also cofounder of the Cuban-Hebrew Congregation on South Beach in 1961. (Courtesy of Norma Orovitz.)

Seen in the photograph above is Temple Moses. Founded in the 1960s by Sephardi Cuban Jewish refugees and led by Solomon Garazi, this large complex in North Beach contains a striking interior. A plaque near the entrance explains: "We will never forget what we left behind on the island of Cuba." Services are conducted in Hebrew and English; prayers are also in Ladino. Many food items served at social gatherings are Middle Eastern in origin. (Courtesy Trevor Green.)

Rabbi Leon Kronish came to Miami Beach during World War II. A former student of Rabbi Stephen Wise, a Zionist leader and a national advocate for the Jewish community and civil rights, by the late 1960s Kronish had achieved national and international prominence in Washington and Israel. Kronish (right) is shown here with Pres. Gerald Ford in 1978, one year after Ford left the White House. (Courtesy Temple Beth Sholom.)

Joe's Stone Crab Restaurant, founded by Joe and Jennie Weiss in 1913 as a lunch counter, grew quickly after it added stone crabs to its menu in the 1920s. By the 1930s, the restaurant was in a new home immediately west of the original location. In the 1980s, the restaurant added a new entranceway from Washington Avenue, a take-out facility called Joe's Take Away, and a new bar and dining area immediately north of the complex, seen here in this late-1960s image. (Courtesy Florida State Archives.)

As Miami Beach's Jewish population soared in the 1960s and 1970s, many Jews moved north along Collins Avenue past 163rd Street. During that era, the area was known as "Motel Row" (today's Sunny Isles Beach), and many of the colorful motels were owned and operated by Jews. Wolfie Cohen's Rascal House Restaurant on Collins Avenue at Northeast 172 Street opened and offered the same delicious deli fare as Cohen's other restaurants in South Beach. (Courtesy of Larry Wiggins.)

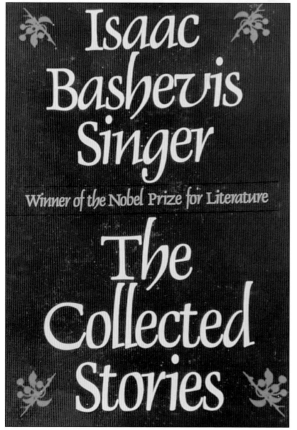

Isaac Bashevis Singer lived on Miami Beach, which provided the setting for a few of his short stories. He and his wife, Alma, also lived in Surfside, abutting the northern border of the city of Miami Beach. While dining at Sheldon's Drugs, their favorite Surfside spot, Singer learned in 1978 that he had won the Nobel Prize for Literature. (Courtesy of Paul S. George.)

The Cinema Theater at 1035 Washington Avenue opened in 1935 as the French Casino, a supper and vaudeville club featuring cabaret acts and showgirls. Converted to a movie theater and renamed the Cinema Casino Theater, it highlighted a stunning Art Deco interior with an auditorium for 1,000 patrons. By the 1970s, it was renamed the Cinema Theater and functioned as a Yiddish theater drawing in the elderly Jewish residents of the neighborhood. With the revival of the Art Deco District, it morphed into a hot nightclub spot for the young and beautiful, including Club Z, the entertainer Prince's Glam Slam, and the popular Mansion. (Courtesy Trevor Green.)

The mid-1950s building housing the headquarters of the Miami Design Preservation League appears in this photograph. Sitting on the bustling crossroads of the Art Deco District—Ocean Drive, Tenth Street, and Barbara Capitman Drive—the league was organized in 1976 by Barbara Capitman, Leonard Horowitz, and others to showcase and preserve the tarnished Art Deco hotels and apartments of South Beach. Since the late 1970s, the league has sponsored walking tours along Ocean Drive and in Lummus Park, just north of Beth Jacob. In 1979, the Miami Design Preservation League was responsible for the national designation of that area as the Miami Beach Architectural District. To the left of the building in this photograph stands the historic marker recounting the fruitful life of Barbara Capitman, the grand dame of the Art Deco District. (Courtesy Trevor Green.)

Six

MODERN-DAY JEWISH EXPERIENCE ON MIAMI BEACH

Kenneth Treister, a brilliant architect who resided on Miami Beach as a youth, designed this world-renowned Holocaust Memorial sculpture. The idea for the memorial can be traced to the mid-1980s when Helen Fagin, a Warsaw ghetto survivor, along with others, were inspired by the more than 20,000 survivors of the Holocaust living on the beach. Clinging to the four-story outstretched hand pointing to the sky are hundreds of small human figures desperately reaching out to one another. A memorial wall wraps around three sides of the sculpture. Elie Wiesel, a Holocaust survivor speaking at the dedication ceremony, explained that "the tragedy which this museum is trying to integrate is beyond words, and beyond imagination, but not beyond memory." (Courtesy Trevor Green.)

Nobel laureate and Holocaust survivor Elie Wiesel is surrounded by well-wishers amid a visit to Miami Beach in the early 1980s. Wiesel chronicled his story in many books, including *Night*, a work based on his experiences as a Jewish prisoner in Auschwitz, which especially resonated with the elderly Jews of Miami Beach, many of whom were Holocaust survivors. Wiesel was a snowbird and had a condominium on the beach. (Courtesy of HistoryMiami Museum.)

Pictured from left to right are former opera singer Cantor Steven Haas and Rabbi Gary Glickstein, seen here honing their pipes while traveling on a bus with Temple confirmation youths on their annual trip to Israel and the Middle East during the Oslo Accords in the 1990s. (Courtesy Temple Beth Sholom.)

Seen here is the Jaime Bronsztein Band providing for a wedding party with klezmer music on Miami Beach in 1985. Klezmer, a Yiddish term, refers to an instrumental musical tradition of the Ashkenazi Jews of Central and Eastern Europe that was often played at celebrations like weddings. Klezmer is also Jewish folk music, and it had a wildly enthusiastic audience on Miami Beach. (Courtesy Florida Memory.)

Pictured above is an example of male Chassidic dancing at Mordechai Korf's bar mitzvah on Miami Beach in the mid-1980s. Male Chassidic, or Hasidic Judaism, is an 18th-century Jewish spiritual revival movement born in western Ukraine that grew more popular and robust in the late 20th century through Chabad epicenters. These mini communities are very religious and represent Orthodox Judaism. There are several on Miami Beach. (Courtesy Florida Memory.)

Mark Alschuler's bar mitzvah, the rite of passage for a 13-year-old Jewish boy, is pictured with Rabbi Leon Kronish in May 1981. In the Jewish tradition, the bar mitzvah boy is now a full member of the community and is responsible for following the mitzvot (commandments). (Courtesy Temple Beth Sholom.)

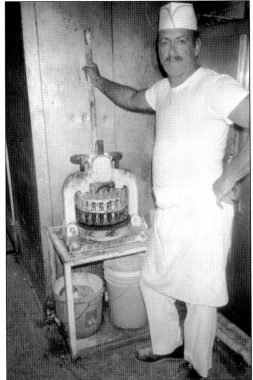

Here, Howard Goren standing by a bagel press in the mid-1980s. Located on South Beach, Goren and Sons Bakery was a Jewish mainstay on Miami Beach for several decades with a loyal clientele. It held a special appeal for many of the neighborhood's elderly residents of the 1970s and 1980s. (Courtesy Florida Memory.)

Rabbi Gary Glickstein, standing in the center of the third row, is seen here accompanying the temple's most recent confirmation class on a trip to Israel in 1986. This annual excursion of the confirmation class to Israel has been a prominent staple of the synagogue's offerings, introduced as an annual ritual by Rabbi Kronish in the 1970s. (Courtesy Temple Beth Sholom.)

Employing heavy doses of wisdom and affability, Rabbi Gary Glickstein appealed to all members of the congregation, including its youngest members, during his long tenure as its senior rabbi. Rabbi Glickman served the congregation in that position from the mid-1980s until the second decade of the 21st century. (Courtesy Temple Beth Sholom.)

Diane Camber holds a certificate of appreciation from Dade County commissioner Barry Schreiber (left) and Mayor Steve Clark (right) for bringing the Jewish Prague historical exhibit, Precious Legacy, to Miami Beach. Diane Camber was the long-serving director of the Bass Museum in South Beach and a progressive force in the community. An art historian, educator, and preservationist, she personally curated many exhibitions in the Bass Museum, including those treating the topics of Art Nouveau and Art Deco as well as the drawings, prints, and works of Frank Lloyd Wright in Florida. Camber was an early supporter and proselytizer behind the movement for the preservation and designation of Miami Beach's world-famous Art Deco District in the 1970s and 1980s. (Courtesy Florida Memory.)

Stephen Muss is seen here in 1985 in front of his newest Seacoast Tower apartment building. A native of New York City, Steve, as he was often called, joined his father in establishing the Alexander Muss & Sons real estate development firm, which constructed more than 25,000 single-family homes in New York. In 1962, the Muss family moved to Miami Beach and developed the Seacoast Towers, along with other residential buildings on the beach and elsewhere in the area. In 1978, he purchased the tarnished Fontainebleau Hotel, renovated it, and engaged Hilton Hotels Corporation to manage the property. Muss and his family were major benefactors to Jewish institutions, including Miami Beach's Temple Emanu-El. (Courtesy of HistoryMiami Museum.)

Tony Goldman is seen in this photograph semi-sprawled across a vintage car with the storied Park Central Hotel standing tall in the background around the 1990s. Coming to Miami Beach with a track record of restoring neighborhoods such as New York City's So Ho, Goldman fixed his eyes on the Art Deco District, whose buildings had fallen into serious decline by the mid-1980s. As he explained, "I took a left turn off Fifth Street and onto Ocean Drive. I got out of my car, saw the Park Central (just two blocks north of Fifth Street on Ocean Drive) and felt like I had fallen upon King Solomon's mines." Goldman purchased the Park Central Hotel and numerous other properties in South Beach, restoring and expanding them by adding restaurants and bars. Within a few years after Goldman's discovery of South Beach, the rejuvenation of the Art Deco District, a national architectural and historic district, was underway. (Courtesy Goldman Properties.)

This bust of Barbara Capitman, the leader of Miami Beach's Art Deco movement, was executed by her mother, the artist Myrtle (Bachrach) Baer, when Barbara was 19 years old in 1939. The bust sits in Lummus Park across from the Cardozo Hotel, the Art Deco District's first restored hostelry, once owned by Barbara Capitman and her sons. (Courtesy Trevor Green.)

Seen here are a somber Barbara Capitman (left) with fellow preservationist Mattie Bower (right) after the bitter loss of the Senator Hotel. The struggle to preserve the hostelry stretched throughout the year 1988 until the demolition was completed near year's end. Capitman seemingly never recovered from this defeat, dying less than two years later at age 69. (Courtesy HistoryMiami Museum.)

Freidman's Kosher Bakery, a landmark in Miami Beach, was located in an Art Deco building designed in 1934 by E.L. Robertson, near the corner of Washington Avenue and Seventh Street. A sign in front of the bakery announced, "Fresh baking All Day—Bread, Challahs, Rolls, Cake." The bakery was still operating in the 1980s, when Leonard Horowitz and Barbara Capitman used the Art Deco building to test a new color scheme, which Horowitz called the "Miami Color Palette." (Courtesy Trevor Green.)

Miami Beach's prominent Wolfson family included Mitchell Wolfson, the first Jewish mayor of the community, as well as his son Mitchell "Mickey" Wolfson Jr. The latter created, with his collection of art work, books, and other objects exhibited in the Wolfsonian, his namesake museum on South Beach, the premier repository of the decorative and propaganda arts bridging the years 1880–1945. (Courtesy of Trevor Green.)

Seen in the photograph are, from left to right, Judge Irving Cypen, Hazel Cypen, and Laura and Paul George in 1991 at a Miami Beach dinner honoring the preeminent supporters of the Miami Jewish Home and Hospital for the Aged (today's Miami Jewish Health). The Cypens, who were Miami Beach residents, were the moving forces behind the Miami Jewish Home and Hospital for the Aged for more than 50 years. (Courtesy Paul S. George.)

The Nelson family has played a significant role in the development of Beth Jacob and Miami Beach for three generations. Ted (left) served as the mayor of Bay Harbor Islands and Beth Jacob's attorney in its later years as a congregation. His son Jonathan (right) grew up on the beach, taught at Miami Beach High, and is president of Beth Jacob. Ted's wife, Sarah "Suki" stands between them, pictured in 1998. (Courtesy Jonathan Nelson.)

Pictured are, from left to right, Harold, Leonard, and Irving Miller, who were principals in Lennar Homes, one of America's premier home builders for 70 years, with Rabbi Gary Glickstein (far right) in the early 2000s. The Miller family members have been generous supporters of Temple Beth Sholom as well as important members of the lay leadership of the congregation. (Courtesy Temple Beth Sholom.)

Stuart Blumberg's biography echoes the stories of many Jewish residents of Miami Beach. His family migrated from New York to Miami Beach in the expansive period following World War II for both reasons of health and economics. Blumberg was the long-term president of the Greater Miami & The Beaches Hotel Association, which promoted Miami Beach as the "Sun and Fun Capital of the World." (Courtesy Stuart Blumberg.)

Gayle Pomerantz, current rabbi at Temple Beth Sholom, is the first woman rabbi in the temple's history. In 2006, Rabbi Pomerantz launched the Open Tent, a Jewish engagement initiative to make Judaism accessible to Jews outside of the physical synagogue. Jewish childbirth classes, arts programs, and an organic food collective, among other programs, have reached thousands. (Courtesy Temple Beth Sholom.)

The Home Instruction for Parents of Preschool Youngsters (HIPPY) began in Miami in 1985 under the wings of Nan Rich and Henry Green. HIPPY is a home visitation program that focuses on parent-involved and -directed early learning for at-risk minority populations, and it grew tremendously under the tutelage of First Lady Hillary Clinton. Author Henry Green and Hillary Clinton are seen in the above photograph at a Miami Beach HIPPY event. (Courtesy of Henry A. Green.)

Pictured with Israeli prime minister Shimon Peres in 1996 is a Florida politician and board member of the United States Holocaust Memorial Museum, Nan Rich. Rich grew up on Miami Beach, attended Temple Beth Sholom, and served as president of the Miami Beach chapter of the National Council of Jewish Woman and as its national president. A tireless advocate for women, children, and Israel, her many leadership roles included minority leader in the Florida Senate. (Courtesy Nany Rich.)

Elderly Miami Beach residents are seen here seated in chairs on the open porch of the Senator Hotel, an Art Deco jewel built in 1939 at 1201 Collins Avenue. The Senator Hotel fell to the wrecking ball in 1988 despite the impassioned efforts of Barbara Capitman and other preservationists. (Courtesy HistoryMiami Museum.)

Congresswoman Ileana Ros-Lehtinen (left) is touring the Iraqi Jewish exhibit at the Jewish Museum of Florida-FIU in 2016. Hillel Shohet is pointing to himself in his class picture before he became a refugee and was displaced from his homeland. Representative Ros-Lehtinen then presented Shohet's story from the floor of the House of Representatives, just as she recounted her own story as a Cuban refugee. (Courtesy Sephardi Voices.)

DISCOVER THOUSANDS OF LOCAL HISTORY BOOKS FEATURING MILLIONS OF VINTAGE IMAGES

Arcadia Publishing, the leading local history publisher in the United States, is committed to making history accessible and meaningful through publishing books that celebrate and preserve the heritage of America's people and places.

Find more books like this at
www.arcadiapublishing.com

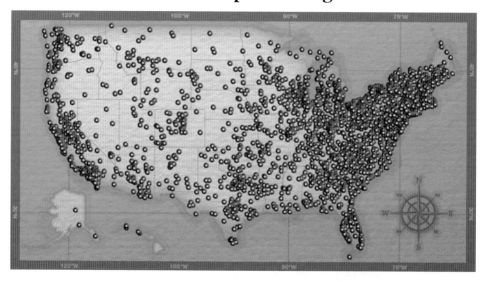

Search for your hometown history, your old stomping grounds, and even your favorite sports team.